Look at Me!

Alicia Dudley
Photography by
Alice McBroom

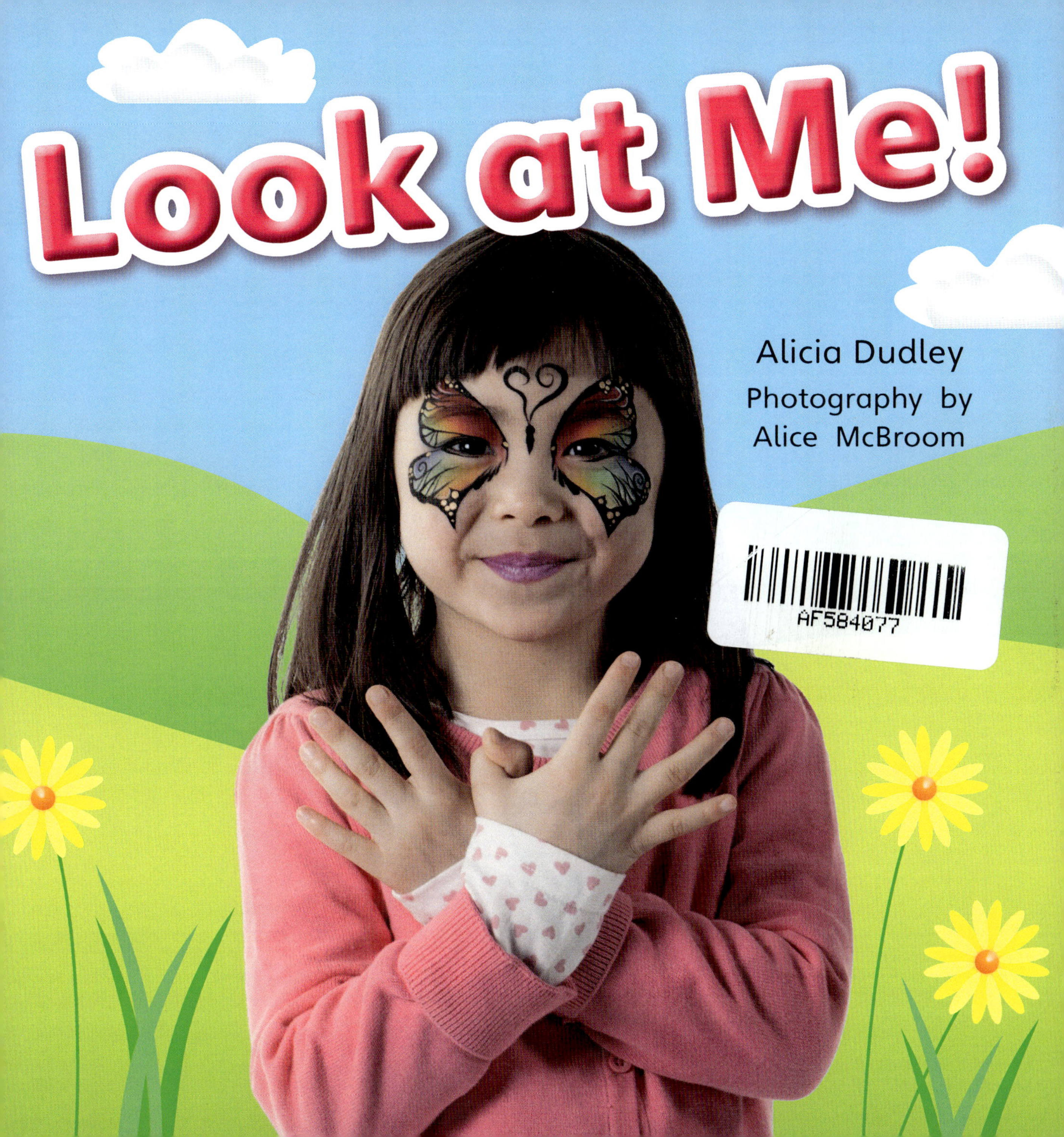

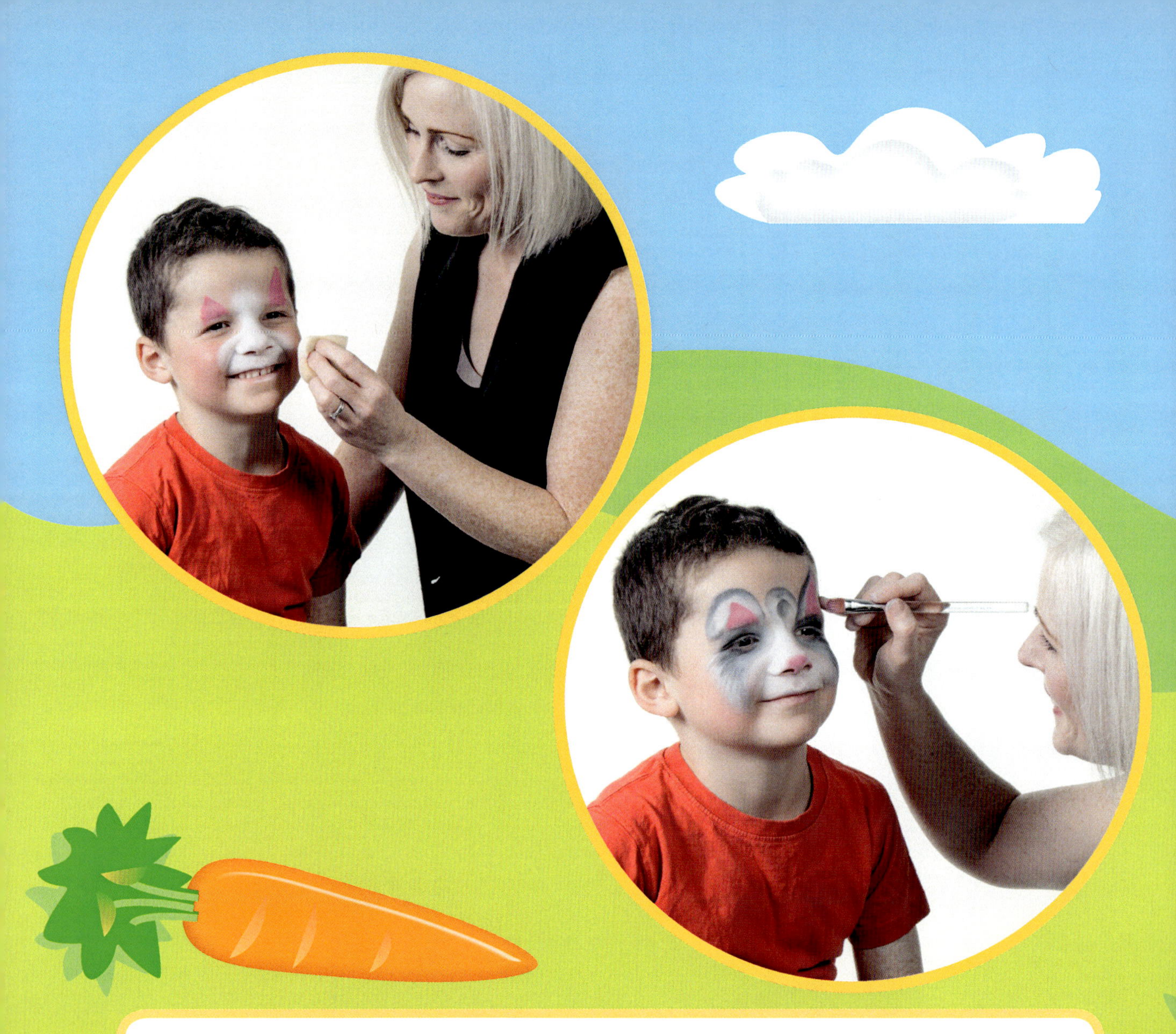

Look at me!

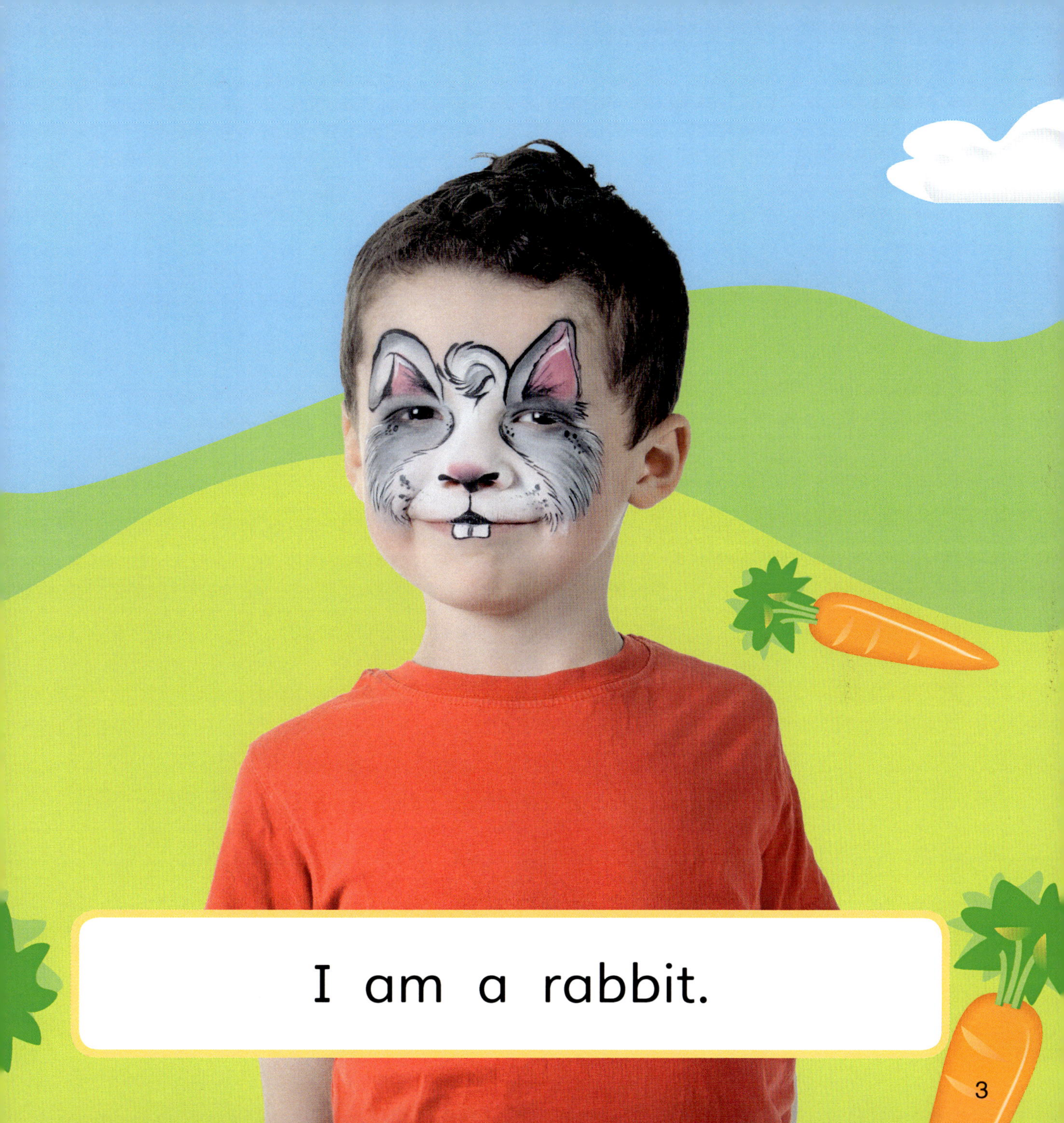

I am a rabbit.

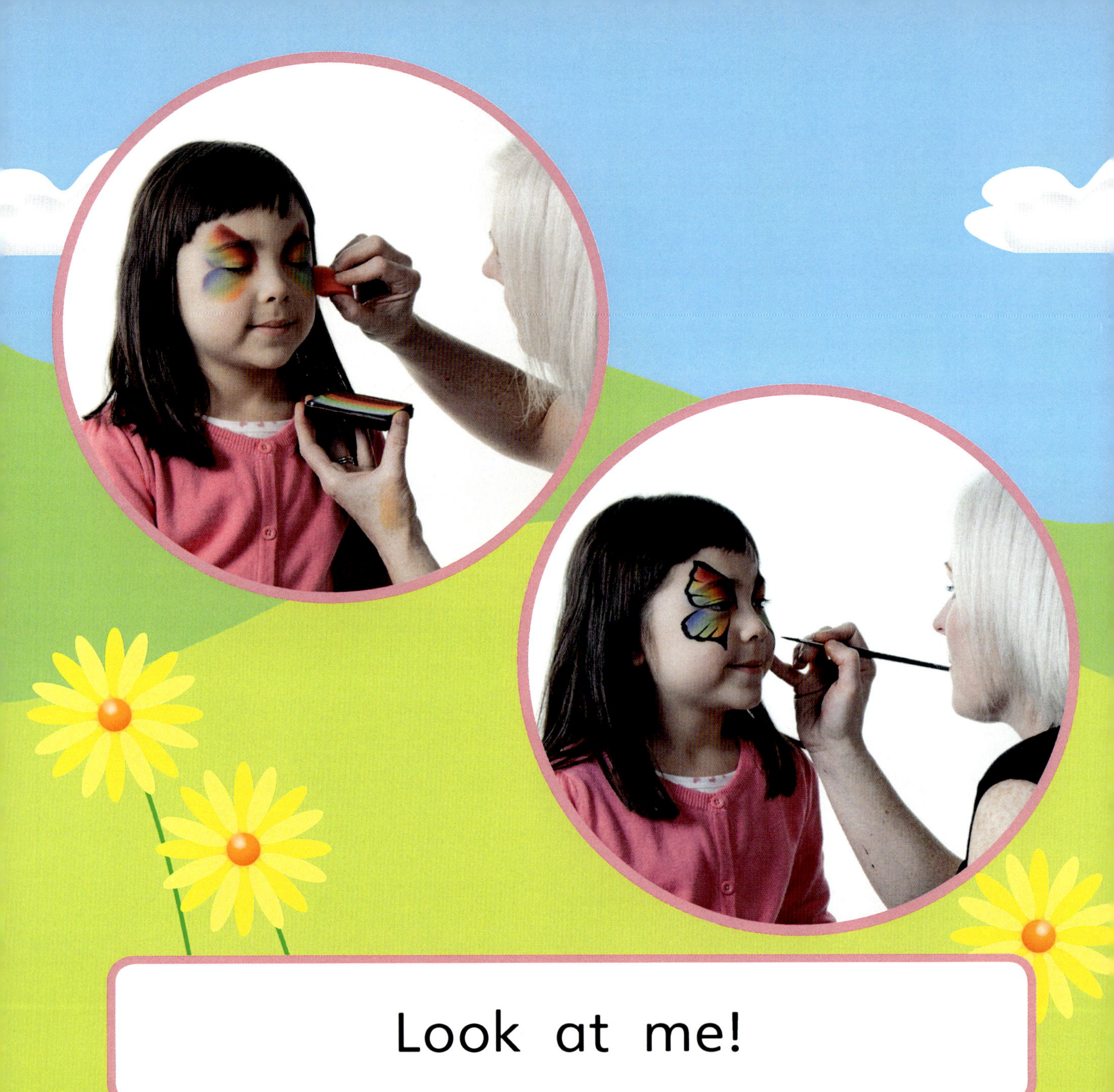

Look at me!

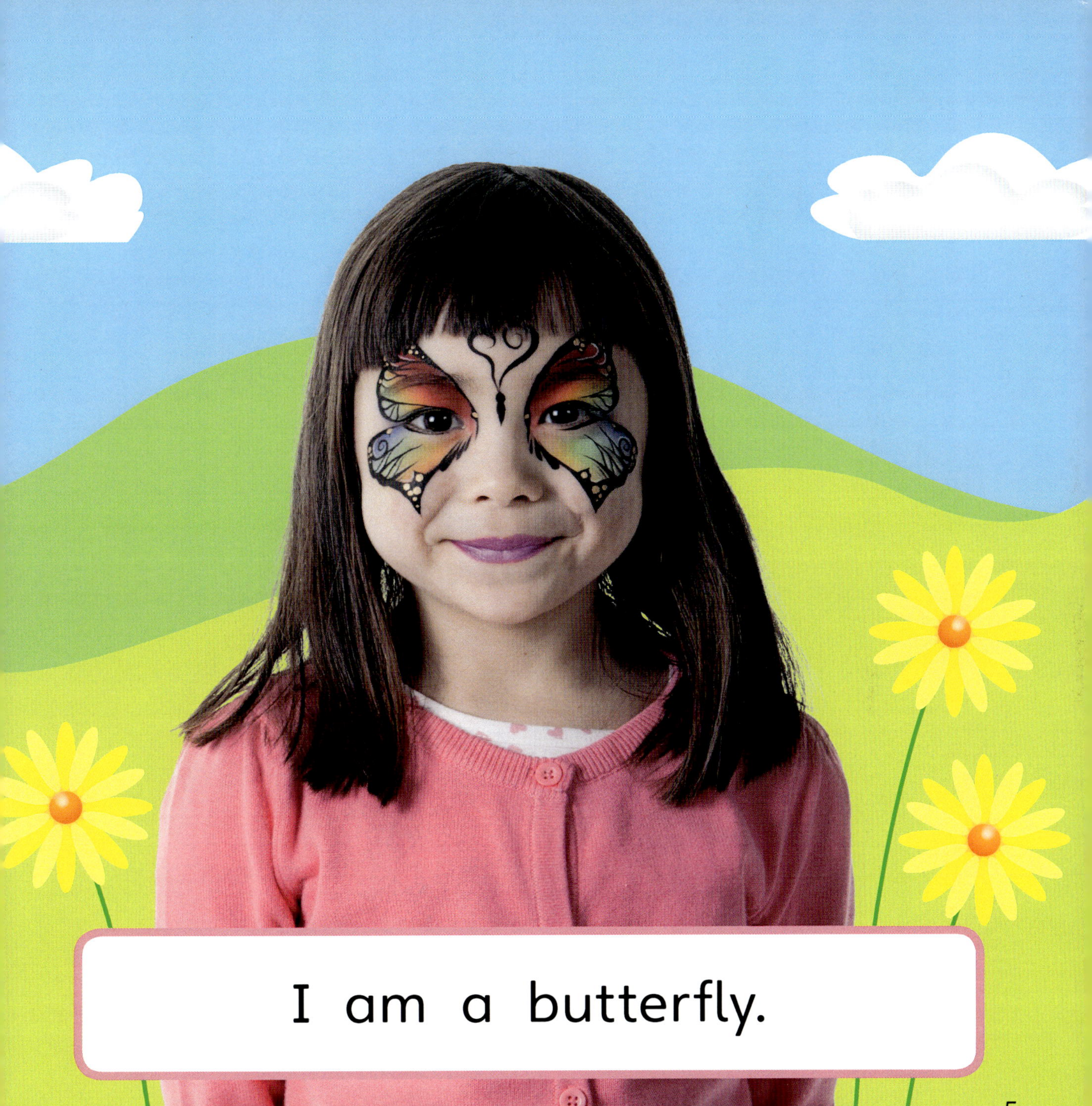

I am a butterfly.

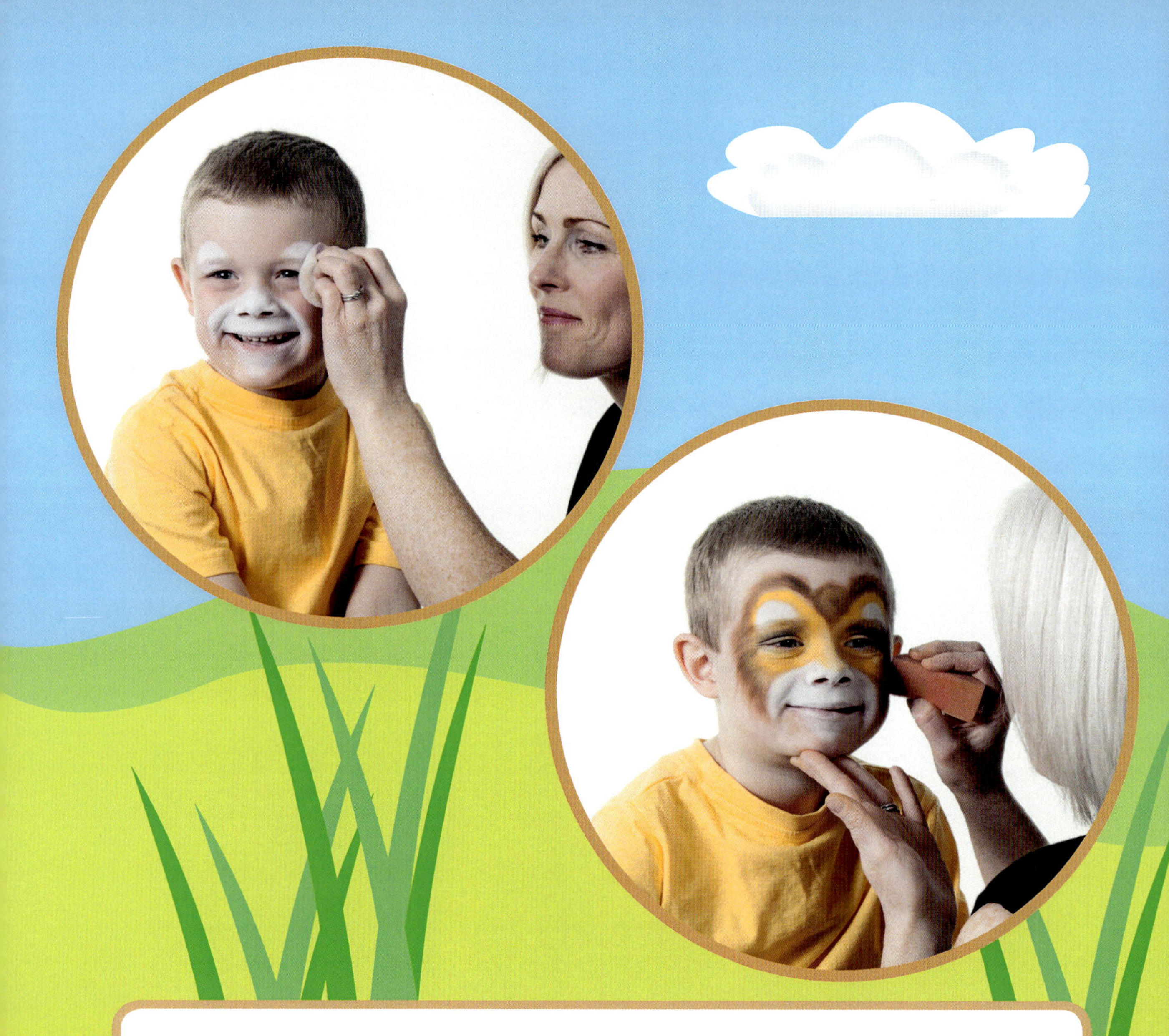

Look at me!

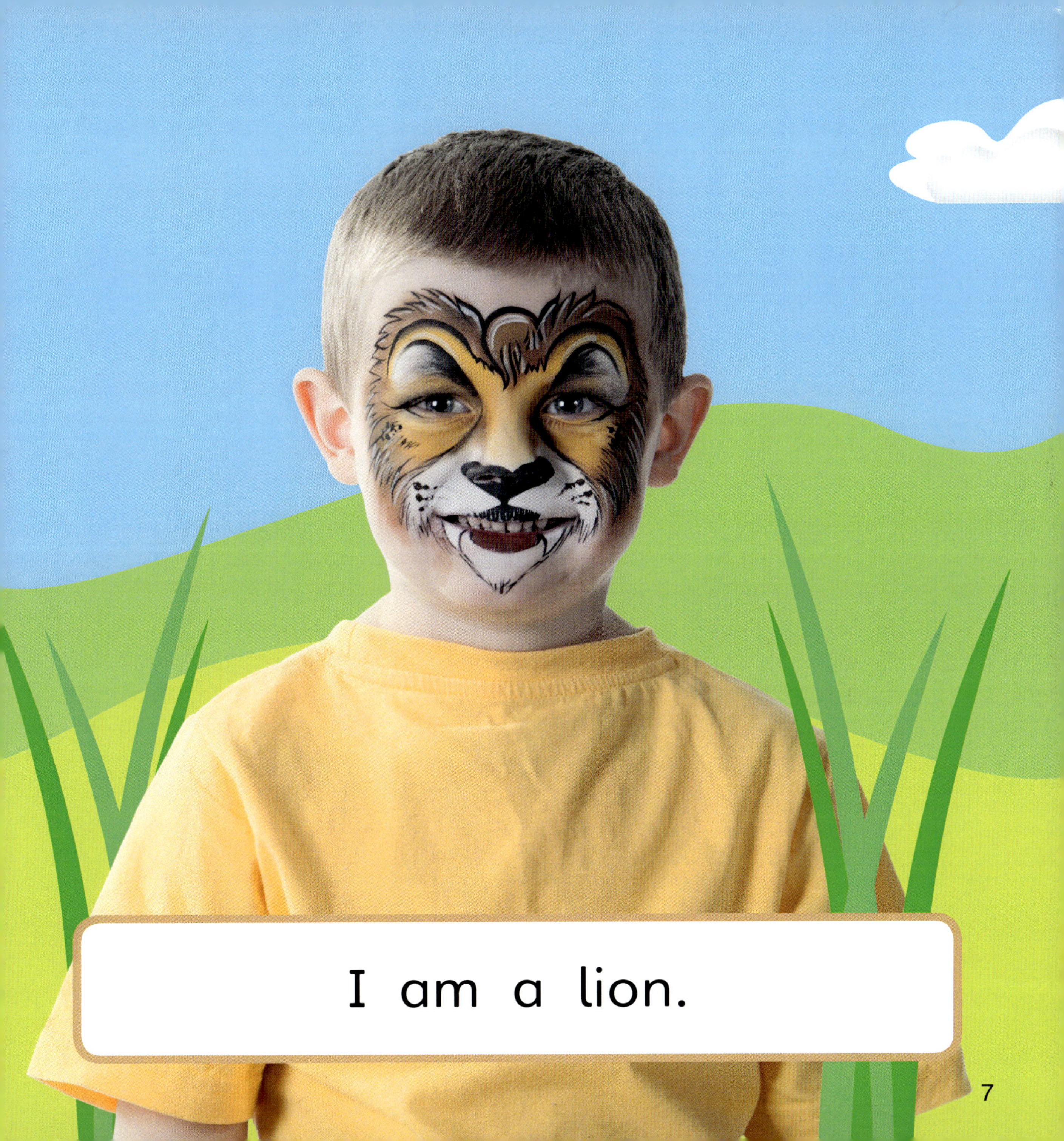

I am a lion.

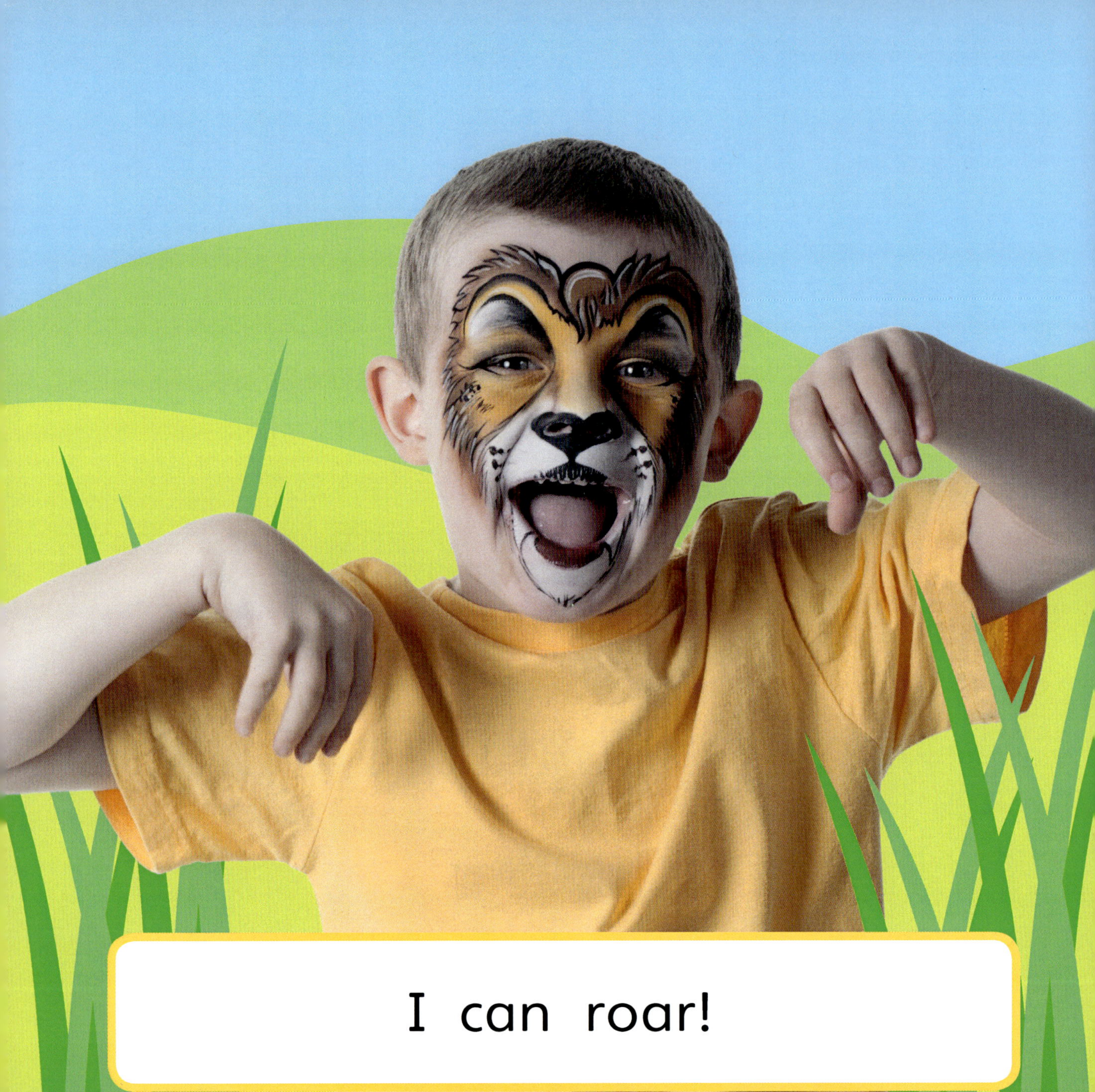

I can roar!